The Art of Conscious Aging *Workbook*

A Guide to Happiness, Health and Purpose in Life's Third Act

By Wayne Robert Lehrer

THE ART OF CONSCIOUS AGING WORKBOOK

First Printing 2024

Conscious Aging Publishing
811 Franklin St.
Santa Monica, CA. 90403
Waynelehrer.com

ISBN 978-2-35689-566-0 (paperback)

Printed in the United States of America

If you would like to learn more about ***The Art of Conscious Aging***, explore Life Coaching or Conscious Aging Coaching or receive information on Workshops, Retreats and our other events and offerings, please visit us at www.waynelehrer.com

Or feel free to contact us directly at info@waynelehrer.com

www.waynelehrer.com

CONTENTS

INTRODUCTION

Aging is a journey we all must undertake, but it is often accompanied by the illusion of immortality in our youth, only to be confronted later in life by the undeniable reality of our own mortality. The Art of *Conscious Aging* invites us to awaken from this illusion and embrace the responsibilities and gifts that come with *conscious aging.*

This phase is not just about accepting the aging process but also about finding joy, fulfillment, and purpose. Aging is not merely the end of something; it is the beginning of a transformative phase filled with potential for inner peace, authentic happiness, a meaningful purpose and self-actualization.

What Does It Mean to Age Consciously?

Conscious Aging means welcoming the good and bad parts of getting older. It's about accepting that things will change as we enter our later years. This view pushes us to learn new abilities, mindsets, and drives to make *the rest of our life the best of our life.* Many people find the shift into the "*Third Act*" confusing. It is often accompanied by an identity crisis, health issues, and emotional turmoil. Yet *Conscious Aging* sees these hurdles as chances to grow and know ourselves better. It teaches us to age with grace, thankfulness, and a lasting sense of purpose.

Facing The Realities of Aging

In *The Art of Conscious Aging,* I describe how my transition into my Third Act forced me to confront the changes growing older was demanding I find answers to. Despite having lived a life of relatively good health, regular exercise, and personal achievement, when I hit 65, I found myself continually confronted with new issues that made the reality that I was aging undeniable. In addition to the initial physical challenges came emotional and personal hurdles—facing mortality, experiencing depression, and feeling almost totally unprepared for all the changes that lay ahead. I knew I had to find a way to make it through what I have come to understand as my personal *Third Act Identity Crisis* if I was going to have any chance of thriving in the years that lay ahead.

A day comes when each of us must face and make peace with the issues of aging. Only as we embrace this process will we discover the extraordinary opportunities that still await us.

With thought provoking questions, opportunities for self-reflection and the invitation to clarify the personal values and purpose of your Third Act, *The Art of Conscious Aging Workbook* will guide you through the ways and means to make this life changing transition and assist you in *A Guide to Happiness, Health and Meaning in Life's Third Act.*

The Purpose of This Workbook

This *workbook* aims to help you grasp the concepts of *Conscious Aging* outlined in the original book. By dividing each chapter into thoughtful questions, hands-on activities, and reflective moments, you can map out your path into and through your *Third Act.*

Each section of the *workbook* will:

- Encourage reflection on how aging has impacted your life.
- Help you develop new perspectives on aging and offer tools to deal with its challenges.
- Inspire you to embrace your *Third Act* with intention and joy.
- Clarify how and where you are being offered opportunities to grow and change.
- Reveal your path, define your Third Act values and motivate you to chart your course.

How to Use This Workbook

This *workbook* will help you through the later parts of life as you work with the ideas of *Conscious Aging* in a hands-on, thoughtful way. You'll find insights and steps you can take, along with exercises that let you use these ideas in your everyday life. As you read each chapter, you'll get chances to think about how you're aging now and find new ways to grow, change, and live more purposefully.

Each Chapter Follows A Consistent Structure:

Introduction to Key Concepts: Every chapter starts by discussing key principles about *Conscious Aging*. These introductions lay the groundwork for grasping the significance of each theme—be it releasing old attachments, nurturing gratitude, or finding new purpose.

Reflective Questions: After each section, you'll find a set of thought-provoking questions designed to help you connect the chapter's themes and ideas with your life stories. These questions are key in deepening your grasp of these ideas and pointing you toward their practical application. Don't rush through them; write down your thoughts as you go. Exercises that make you think are some of the best tools to learn about yourself. They let you spot patterns, gain insights, and have realizations that might not be clear immediately.

Action Steps: Each chapter ends with one or more steps to ensure you put what you've learned into practice. These tasks might involve setting up routines, writing about specific topics, letting go of old roles, or building new relationships. These exercises aim to bring the ideas about *Conscious Aging* into your day-to-day life, making sure that these changes happen in your heart, mind and your life.

Keeping Tabs on Your Journey: Many chapters have tools to track your progress and opportunities to reflect and then put into action. These tools help you monitor how you're growing over time. You'll clearly understand how you're changing by noting down your thoughts, actions, and feelings. Make sure to look back at these tracking exercises now and then to see how far you've come and to tweak your goals as you move ahead.

How to Approach the Workbook:

Take Your Time: I now know that growing older with purpose isn't a race; it's a journey of growth. You can spend as many days as you like to finish each chapter in the book. Some sections might demand deeper thought and confront uncomfortable feelings, while others might be simpler to grasp or put into practice. The key is to be kind and give yourself enough time to process and understand these ideas.

Journal Often: This *workbook* becomes more useful when paired with daily writing. It will help to keep a separate paper notebook or Word document where you'll jot down your thoughts, answers to the reflective questions, and notes about the action steps. Your journal will grow into a record of your *Conscious Aging* journey and the changes and insights you might have along the way.

Take Another Look at the Exercises: What you face at a certain age will be different from what you meet at another time in life. It is good practice to look at some of the reflective questions or action points after a few months as you may get a different thinking perspective. You can expect to notice changes in your experiences regarding these exercises as you age.

Connect with Others: If you can, talk about these experiences with someone you trust, like a friend, partner, or group going through *Conscious Aging* together. Sharing the ideas and tasks from the *Workbook* with others will give you new perspectives and boost your understanding. Also, speaking with others will help you feel less alone with your thoughts and feeling, which, in turn, will make these changes easier to adopt and apply.

By the end of this *Workbook*, you will have explored multiple dimensions of *Conscious Aging*—physical, emotional, spiritual, and relational. You will have created a roadmap for living the rest of your life with newfound intention, joy, and serenity. I wish you a thoughtful, insightful and joyous journey as you set out on this path toward Self-Actualization.

CHAPTER 1

THE ART OF CONSCIOUS AGING

Getting older is often perceived as a downward slope, with many thinking of it as a slow, quiet fade into life's later years. But The Art of *Conscious Aging* shows a different view. It presents getting older as an invitation to renew and change, a time full of opportunities to grow, change and fulfill your infinite potential. The premise of *Conscious Aging* is that life occurs in three distinct stages: *Act One*, *Act Two*, and *Act Three*. Each stage has its themes and events, leading you to an ever-changing and ever-increasing understanding of who you are and where you are going.

THE FIRST ACT: LEARNING, GROWTH, AND DISCOVERY

The First Act of life goes from birth to early adulthood. During this time, we show curiosity, explore our world, and develop ourselves. As kids and young adults, we yearn to learn more about the world, find out what we're good at, and figure out who we are in it. This stage brings big changes, both in body and mind. As young people we spend our time learning about ourselves, what's around us, and what we can do.

This stage is full of wonder and the itch to explore the world around us. We put ourselves out there and mess up, and by doing this, we pick up key lessons about ourselves. In the First Act, much of life centers on growing and pushing boundaries. Our world is wide open, and anything and everything is possible.

The Second Act: Getting Things Done and Finding Our Place

In this part of life, we are focused on chasing success, stability, and identity. During this time, we work hard to achieve external goals— build careers, start families, and accumulate wealth, property, and prestige. It's when we attempt to figure out our place in the world. We care about what's "ours"—our job, our family, our accomplishments.

In this act, we are mostly focused on the outside world. We spend our time and energy building job skills, raising kids, and helping society. Success often links to real results, like job promotions, awards, and money in the bank. Many see this time as their most productive and successful. But as the Second Act moves on, a wish for something more—something deeper—often begins to impose itself into our life, work, and relationships.

The Third Act: Renewal and Reflection

The Third Act kicks off around the mid-50s and lasts for the rest of life. In the past, people linked this stage with decline—leaving work, cutting back, and seeking comfort. However, The Art of *Conscious Aging* takes issue with this old-fashioned view. Instead, it paints the *Third Act* as a time to start fresh, look back, discover who we want to be "now," and make the necessary changes.

In contrast to the First and Second Acts, which focus on external growth and success, the *Third Act* prompts us to look inside ourselves. This phase allows us to reflect, think about our life experiences, move on from old roles, and welcome new ways to grow. During this time, we ask ourselves big questions like, "Who am I now?" and "How do I want to spend the rest of my life?" These questions help us find new meaning and identity beyond the signs of success we've come to rely on — exclusively — in our First and Second Act.

Rather than viewing the *Third Act* as a time of decline, The Art of *Conscious Aging* sees it as a stage filled with potential. It is an opportunity for satisfaction, stability, and continued growth—both emotionally and spiritually. By consciously engaging with the aging process, individuals can transform this phase of life into one of fulfillment, connection, and meaning. *The Third Act* becomes a time for pursuing passions, deepening relationships, and contributing to the world in new and meaningful ways.

In this act, we switch our attention from "what I've done" to "who I am." We look for ways to grow, start creative projects, or discover new methods to help our communities.

This time involves letting go—of old identities, roles, and what others expect—and accepting a truer, more thoughtful version of ourselves. While many see the *Third Act* as daunting and even terrifying, there is no doubt that thorough the practice of *Conscious Aging* it can lead to extraordinary, life enhancing and transformative changes. It can make the *Rest of Your Life the Best of Your Life.*

The Third Act Identity Crisis

The shift from the Second to the *Third Act* often causes an identity crisis. For 30 to 40 years, many of us have built our lives around our jobs, families, and outward accomplishments. As these roles fade, we might feel scared, unsure, and even depressed. When we try to make sense of our lives without the usual markers of success, we will likely feel isolated or like we've suffered a loss.

This stage resembles a "dark night of the soul," where old ways no longer satisfy, but new paths remain unclear. It's a period to question: "What do I want to do now?" and "What is my purpose?" Finding answers to these questions is crucial in navigating the *Third Act.* The *Third Act* can become life's most fulfilling and rewarding chapter for those ready to accept the uncertainty.

Reflective Questions:

How have the roles and identities you built during your Second Act shaped your sense of self?

What challenges are you facing (and perhaps terrified of) as you transition into the *Third Act* of your life?

Consider how you (might) want to define success and fulfillment at this stage of life?

What new opportunities for growth and transformation do you see in your *Third Act*?

Map Your Three Acts: Take a moment to reflect on your life so far. Draw a timeline and divide it into three sections—your First, Second, and *Third Acts*. In each section, write down your key experiences, approach towards life and achievements. Then, in your *Third Act* section, brainstorm new goals, activities, or purposes that excite you for the future.

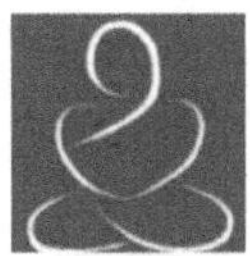

CHAPTER 2

EXERCISING ACCEPTANCE

It's Not Negotiable

Accepting the hard truths about life, such as getting older and dying, is a big part of aging with awareness. In our younger days, we often think nothing can hurt us, so we push our bodies to the max and rarely experience consequences. But as we step into our later years, we see that everything we do has an effect, and we can no longer bargain with the new consequences that aging places in our path — *whether we want to acknowledge them or not.* Getting older shows us that the choices we made when we were younger are no longer applicable, and it's essential, to our *Third Act* well-being that we learn to pay attention, make the appropriate changes and welcome changes as an opportunity and not a limitation.

The Expiration Date

We can't pinpoint the exact day, but one of the toughest facts about getting older is that our physical lives will end at some point. This impending deadline will likely worry and scare us if we haven't come to terms with our own death. *Conscious aging* asks us to face this truth head-on and use it to push ourselves to live on purpose and without looking back with regret. This shift in our thinking helps us zero in on what's important, bringing us to a state of acceptance, inner calm and authentic happiness.

You Are Not Your Story

Many of us have built our identities around the stories we tell about ourselves—whether these tales are about our successes, struggles, or health issues. Yet, as we age, these tales can box us in, keeping us stuck in what's gone by. Growing older with awareness asks us to let go of these old stories, and see ourselves in a new light, and zero in on the here and now and what's yet to come. When we grasp that we're not just the sum of our past tales, we can step into a freer and stronger version of who we are — and write an entirely uplifting and redemptive *Third Act.*

The Gift of Grieving

Growing old brings grief with it. We lose people we care about, our health declines, and parts of who we are change. Grief hurts, but it will also change us for the better. We can face these losses and find new purpose by embracing our grief. The trick is to let ourselves feel the full weight of our sorrow without trying to skip over it or avoid it. When we work through each stage of grief, we open the door to healing, personal growth, and finding hope again.

Reflective Questions:

What parts of getting older do you find the hardest to accept — right now?

____

____

____

____

____

____

How have the choices you made in the past shaped how you're experiencing aging today?

____

____

____

____

____

____

How do you feel about the non-negotiable "reality" of an expiration date? Does it motivate you to make life changes?

____

____

____

____

____

____

What narratives have you created for yourself that (are tired and) no longer serve you?

How can you begin to accept the grieving process for - past regrets, losses, and shortcomings?

Action Step

Grief Inventory: Set aside time to think about the losses you must during your *Third Act.* Create a list of these losses—including physical and mental abilities, opportunities, unfulfilled dreams and un-mended relationships. For each loss, describe its impact on you, what you can learn from it and how to turn it into a growth opportunity. This task will help you begin to face and embrace the grief that has trapped you in stories of "what was" and kept you from writing stories of "all I still can be."

Progress Tracking:

Monthly Grief Reflection: For the coming month, take time each week to check how you're handling grief.

- Jot down the emotional, mental, and physical shifts you spot as you work to accept things. How are your thoughts on getting older changing?
- Are you coming up with new ways to deal with grief and loss, or are you uncovering new wells of strength?

CHAPTER 3

PRACTICING LETTING GO

Learning to Let Go

As we go through the *Third Act*, one of the biggest challenges we face is Letting Go—Letting Go of roles, things we own, what we expect, and even relationships that don't feed or nurture us anymore. We often stick to old ways of living because they make us feel safe, but growing older with awareness pushes us to release what we're attached to and welcome new challenges. The more we hang on to things that no longer work for us, the more we hold back our chances to grow, transform and discover our deeper truer selves.

You're as Sick as Your Secrets

In The Art of *Conscious Aging,* letting go strongly influences releasing emotional burdens, including long-kept secrets and unfinished business. These hidden parts of us—be they past mistakes, regrets, or personal fears—will put an unnecessary strain our mental and emotional health as we traverse life's *Third Act.* Keeping secrets is antithetical to *Conscious Aging* and directly inhibits our ability to enjoy the freedom, peace, and emotional wellness that it promotes.

The Emotional Cost of Secrets

Secrets have a negative influence on every part of our lives when we are consciously or unconsciously hiding them. As time passes, keeping up a front, and carrying the emotional baggage they represent, will stress us out and undermine our best intentions. These secrets might be about old relationships, things we regret but don't say, or long fought inner battles. They stop us from being present. They create emotional blocks making it hard to move on or enjoy life.

Hiding these secrets, from ourselves and others, creates paralyzing guilt, shame, and fear — especially as we age. This emotional stress builds up and cut off from others, resulting in painful isolation, and physical issues like: debilitating tension, deep fatigue, and chronic disease. One of the greatest gifts we can give ourselves, in later life, is to make peace with the past, first by telling ourselves the truth, and then become open, vulnerable and transparent with others. The result of this is a newfound freedom and optimism that elevates our *Third Act* to a time of true renewal.

The Importance of Addressing Unresolved Issues

Facing and dealing with unresolved feelings plays a key role in mindful aging. To let go of our emotional baggage, we must overcome our fears regarding what others will think. It is only by exposing these hidden parts of ourselves that we step out of our old persona and begin to feel alive and free again.

This might mean having tough talks with family and friends, keeping a diary, or getting help from a therapist or counselor. Owning up to, and tackling, these long-held secrets allow us to shed the emotional baggage we've carried for years, make peace between the divisive sides of ourselves and move toward becoming a wholly integrated human being.

Healing and Emotional Freedom

A central idea in The Art of *Conscious Aging* is how letting go can heal us. When we share our secrets —we no longer feel trapped by shame, guilt, or fear about our past and find ourselves accept who we are, practicing loving kindness toward ourselves and others and enjoying a sense of peace and serenity we have never known before.

Living Authentically in the Third Act

Letting go of secrets we've kept for a long time isn't just about lightening our load—it's about being real in our later years. When we stop trying to hide, open up to real connections and discover a deeper feeling of intimacy in all our relationships. Being open with our feelings lets us live more honestly, matching what's inside to what we show the world.

In our golden years, being true to ourselves is essential to discovering the purpose that will give our *Third Act* meaning and value. When we know who we are, and where we are going, we are no longer at the mercy of what others might think. In fact, in embracing our authentic Self, we begin to attract all we need to flourish, meaningful relationships with like-minded people and the knowledge that we are at last being fulfilling our true calling.

Anything Can Happen, Anything

Letting go allows us to see that anything can happen. When we stop trying to control everything, we open ourselves up to new experiences, opportunities, and dynamic spiritual growth. As we enter our *Third Act*, we must keep an open mind and invite the unknown into our life. We might start a new hobby, find new routes across town, or start checking off items on our bucket list. The sky's the limit when we stop trying to manage every little thing and instead let … Any and Every Thing Happen.

Reflective Questions:

What or who are you holding onto that no longer serves you?

What feelings or secrets do you need to face to get on with your life?

Where in your life could you loosen your grip and get a little more adventurous?

What changes do you need to make to begin to believe that Anything is Possible?

ACTION STEP:

Let-Go Ritual: Everyday pick something you've been clinging to that no longer serves you or holds you back. It could be an item, a habit, or a feeling. Write down why you've kept it, what it means to you and why it's time to Let it Go. Then, do something to symbolize this —give it away, share it with someone else or release it by writing, shouting, or burning it. Don't forget to allow yourself feel the lightness that accompanies Letting Go of the old to make room for the You.

Progress Tracking:

Weekly Reflection: Over the next four weeks, watch how your life shifts as you release these old attachments and emotional baggage. Every week, write down any fresh experiences, ideas, or emotions that have popped up since you started to let go. How has this change impacted your outlook, connections, health and optimism?

CHAPTER 4

EMBRACING THE PRESENT

Living in the Here and Now

Conscious aging brings us an amazing gift that allows us to live in the now. When we're younger, we often get caught up in chasing success, focusing on our goals, and always thinking about what's next. This focus on the future can make us anxious, as we're always running after something, while missing what's right in front of us. But as we move into our *Third Act,* we need to pivot and change. Instead of always looking ahead, we can start to pay attention to what's happening right now. After all, the "here and now" is the only place where we are truly alive.

The Art of *Conscious Aging* encourages us to stop always looking ahead and enjoy the beauty, happiness, and purpose we find right now. When we focus on the present, we see how rich life is as it happens. This change from thinking about the future to living in the now helps us let go of the worries, fears, and regrets that most often accompany aging.

As we enter the *Third Act* and realize our days are numbered, we are confronted with a choice — projecting our fears into our future or embracing a chance to Re-Invent ourselves and live a truly unique and deeply satisfying now. Instead of thinking about the past and stressing about what's to come, living in the now lets us enjoy every moment, connection, and emotion we face. We start to notice the little things that make us happy—like talking to someone we care about, feeling the sun on our skin, or just enjoying a peaceful moment.

Transforming How We Perceive Aging

This way of being in the now changes our outlook on getting older. Rather than seeing Aging through the eyes of worry, regret, and worst-case scenarios we view it as a chance to re-connect with our dreams, complete unfinished projects and share love with those we may have let slip out of our lives. The here and now turns into a well of joy as we connect more with what's around us. Growing older with awareness shows us it's not about how many days we have left but how we decide to use each of those days.

When we stop chasing achievements, it is natural that we turn our attention to what really matters to us, to what we would like to contribute and to how we can create value in our life, the lives of those around us, and the world at large. This shift results in a sense of peace and calm, that we are in the right place (at last) at the right time and doing what God put us here to do. We know we're living in line with a higher calling.

Finding Meaning and Joy in Everyday Life

When we live in the present, we find more meaning in our surroundings and relationships. Mindfulness, which means being aware in each moment, helps us see and value things we might miss. At last, we are enjoying the simple things, like a grandchild's laugh, a beautiful sunset, or a quiet time to think. These little moments build up to a life with more depth and satisfaction.

The Power of Gratitude

Gratitude is a powerful way to stay grounded in the present. When we practice gratitude, we turn our attention away from what we lack or what could go wrong and tune into the incredible abundance that surrounds us. This increases our sense of inner peace and heightens our experience of the joy that is "life on life's terms." Hundreds of studies have confirmed that people who express thanks and practice gratitude tend to be healthier, happier, and more positive.

Making a daily list of things we're grateful for is one of the easiest and most effective ways to live in the moment. Whether we think about big blessings or small daily joys, gratitude rewires our brains to view the world through a positive lens of blessings, abundance, and infinite possibilities.

Do New Sh*t

As we age, most of us tend to settle into patterns and shy away from change. Yet living in the now also means welcoming fresh experiences. Stepping out of our safe zone, trying new things, and facing life with wonder will reawaken our enthusiasm, courage and feeling of awe. In our later years, this willingness to try "new sh*t" keeps our spirit young and, once again, live with the joy and curiosity of a child.

Reflective Questions:

How often do you spend time fretting about what's to come and reliving what's passed instead of savoring the now? What form do these thoughts take (disasters, loss, isolation, depression)?

Make a list of the little joys can you cherish right in this minute?

How can you bring more thankfulness into your everyday life?

What's one fresh activity, or experience, you've been putting off, and can jump into today?

Action Step

Gratitude Journal: Begin a daily practice of writing down at least five things you appreciate and are grateful for. Pay attention to both major and minor aspects of your existence, and observe how this new habit shifts your outlook as time passes.

Progress Tracking:

Monthly Presence Check-In:

- When each week ends, take some time to consider how much you managed to stay in the here and now.
- Jot down any instances where you felt present and observe how they affected your day.
- Look over these notes at the month's end and evaluate how your capacity to live in the present has changed.

CHAPTER 5

DEVELOPING BALANCE

The book digs deep into balance as a key part of staying healthy at every age. Balance keeps changing, so we must adjust to life's ups and downs and constant fluctuations — paying special attention to the various parts of our lives, like health, sleep, exercise, friendships, and hobbies. When things get off-kilter, it's time to make some changes to get back on track. When we recognize and embrace the necessity to adapt it becomes a vehicle for mindfulness and powerful force for *Aging Consciously.*

Albert Einstein's famous words, "To keep your balance, you must keep moving," hit the nail on the head. The text explains that *conscious aging* requires constant learning, adjustment, and fine-tuning, just like riding a bike, where you have to keep pedaling or you'll fall. This balance isn't just about staying on your feet; it covers how you feel, think, and connect with your inner self as you age.

The book stresses that awareness of our internal and external environments helps us notice when we lose balance. Realizing this imbalance is the first step in restoring harmony. Take food, for example. If we eat too much today, or the wrong types of food, we will likely feel tired and off our game tomorrow. But if we eat with balance, awareness, and a sensitivity to today's needs, we boost our health and keep our daily routines smooth. This same idea applies to our bonds with others, our jobs, our ability to accomplish our dreams and even how we relax and have fun.

As we age, we must become more aware of how the changes in our bodies, surroundings and relationships affect us and impact our overall sense of balance. My message to people in their "*Third Act*" is to see that balance isn't about keeping things the same but about learning to pay attention to who we are what we need and how are world affects us and then learning to make the requisite changes and adjustments quickly, gracefully, and efficiently.

When we age with purpose, the path to balance becomes a deliberate choice, the promise we make to take care of ourselves, and the understanding that finding equilibrium is an ongoing, process that requires constant tweaking and attention. As we become committed to living with balance as a primary focus, the payoffs are enormous, the pitfalls minimalized, and greater awareness and sensitivity to every aspect of life.

Morning Rituals

Morning rituals have a powerful influence on our ability to establish and re-establish balance throughout the rest of the day. Meditation prayer, stretching, or reading - these rituals help to create clarity and give us purpose. When we start the day with intention, we set up a peaceful and focused mindset, which makes it easier to maintain balance as life throws us curveballs. A morning ritual, that's just for you, is essential to flourish in the midst of life's ups and downs.

Meditation and Mindfulness

Meditation helps us stay balanced by smoothing life's bumps and potholes, release stress and connect us to our own Higher Power — the "still small voice within." It allows us to watch our thoughts and feelings, without trying to control them. It enhances our belief we live in a primarily benevolent world. When we practice mindfulness - focusing on the present moment - we face life with greater clarity, calmness and equanimity. If we meditate daily, we tend to stay grounded, no matter what challenges *Aging* throws our way.

Reflective Questions:

How balanced do you feel in your day-to-day life?

Which parts of your life seem off-kilter, why, and what can you do about it?

How will you work meditation and awareness into your daily routine?

Describe what a balanced life will look like … for you … right now?

Action Step

Create a Morning Routine:

- Think about what you need to feel centered and balanced when your day begins.
- Develop a morning routine that combines spiritual, mental, and physical activities.
- Try meditation, reading, stretching, journaling, and identifying how blessed you are.
- Change your routine, as needed, to match your activities, needs and priorities.
- Start a daily grateful practice by listing 5-10 things and sharing then with a friend.

Progress Tracking

Balance Journal: Record how balanced you feel each day over the next month. Note which activities or habits enhance your ability to maintain and come back into balance and which throw you off. At the week's end, look for any patterns you spot. Use these observations to adjust your routine and practices to maintain better balance in the week that follows and continue this practice.

CHAPTER 6

THE IMPORTANCE OF SELF-CARE

As we grow older, self-care impacts our lives and well-being in every way. It's more than just how you treat yourself; it includes habits that keep your mind, emotions, and body ship-shape. In our *Third Act*, looking after ourselves isn't negotiable - it's a must do.

Self-Care is an ongoing practice that becomes a moving target as we age — requiring constant and continuous thought, awareness, and loving-kindness if we wish to Thrive. It involves doing "whatever it takes" to connect with our spiritual and emotional core, which in turn trains us to effortlessly adapt to the many challenges that accompany aging with a calm heart, clear mind steady courage and resilient spirit.

Use It or Lose It

Taking care of our physical health becomes vital as we enter our later years. Our bodies change, so we need to change how we keep ourselves strong and alert. Moving and working out, even if it's just easy stretches or walks, are an everyday necessity. The saying "use it or lose it" rings true here, since muscles, flexibility, and energy often dissipate and weaken with age. Sticking to an active routine will go a long way to keep the grim reaper at bay.

As we age, exercise doesn't have to be tough, overly long, or exhausting; it just needs to happen often and should be stimulating, uplifting and fun. It's really as simple as doing some yoga in the morning, going for an energetic walk, or lifting light weights. It is also choosing to take the stairs instead of the elevator, parking a little farther away and often going for it when your brain tells you, "I don't wanna!" The main thing is, keep moving and challenging yourself. Use it or Lose it!

Nutrition: The Food You Eat Shapes Who and How You Are

In *Conscious Aging,* nutrition has a crucial impact on maintaining our health, energy, and overall wellness. As we age, our bodies need specific nutrients that require careful consideration. The foods we pick, portion sizes, meal timings, and outlook - each have an even greater effect on our health as we age. The well-known saying, "You are what you eat," becomes even more important as we enter the *Third Act* of our lives where we clearly see the results of our lifelong eating habits … if we are willing to face them.

A central tenet of *Conscious Aging* is the necessity to examine our eating habits, not just our food choices. One example of how to do this exists in the Japanese practice of Hara Hachi. In this ancient practice we are encouraged to eat with an awareness of every bite, mostly what is grown locally and in season and stopping eating when we feel 80% full. These simple shifts in our eating habits will surly help control our caloric intake, prevent us from overeating, boost our digestive health and assist us in extracting the maximum nutritional value from the food we eat.

Another simple rule of thumb is to make a practice of avoiding food that cause inflammation and increase those that do not. Study after study has shown how inflammation is at the center of every kind of health issue (especially when you are older) — joint pain, heart issues, cancer, and memory loss. A basic list of inflammatory foods includes refined sugars, unhealthy fats, processed grains, alcohol and certain veggies.

Ultimately eating isn't about following strict food rules. It's about figuring out what your body needs and making small, lasting changes that help you feel better in the long run. As you notice how different foods affect you - whether they give you a boost or make you feel tired - you can practice *Conscious Aging* by doing your own research. Whether in your own body, with the help of knowledgeable medical professional or with the abundance of wisdom available online you will be empowered to take your health back into your own hands.

Changing Your Diet as Your Needs Change

As we age, our bodies need different nutrients. We need more calcium and vitamin D to keep our bones strong and more fiber to help our digestion work well. We should eat less salt to control our blood pressure and drink plenty of water since we might not feel as thirsty as we used to. When we adjust our diet to meet these new needs, we are better and lower our chances of acquiring even more of the health problems that often accompany aging. Eating well in our later years is about cutting some things out, learning to make smarter choices and ultimately paying closer attention to how what we eat effects who we are.

Reflective Question:

How are you caring for your body, mind, and spirit right now?

Are there aspects and areas, in your life, where you could improve your self-care routine?

How can you add more physical activity, like stretching, walking, or taking the stairs?

What do you know, intellectually and experientially about how the food you are currently eating is influencing your health and well-being?

ACTION STEP

Make a Self-Care Plan:

- Consider the areas in life where you need to practice better/more responsible self-care.
- Create a personal plan that includes exercise, relaxation, meditation, and a healthy diet.
- Start small—maybe with a walk each day or yoga once a week—and grow from there.

Progress Tracking

Self-Care Journal:

- Over the next month, start a self-care journal.
- Daily, write down what you do to care for your body, mind, and spirit.
- Think about how these activities affect you—do they give you more energy, help you think clearer, and improve your mood?
- At the end of every week, look back at what you've done and change your plan if needed.

CHAPTER 7

THE POWER OF RELATIONSHIPS IN AGING

As we enter our *Third Act*, we become increasingly aware of how much our relationships matter— our bonds with our family, friends, and communities. In our later years, the nature of our relationships shifts. They may no longer revolve around work, competition, sports or targeted goals but now center on shared values, emotional intimacy, being of service, common causes, soul pleasures and simply keeping each other company. Building and strengthening these connections is key to our quality of life in our *Third* Act.

In The Art of *Conscious Aging*, I took time to discuss how the strength of our relationships impacts our joy, health, and longevity. Studies backs this up, showing that people with solid social circles have fewer physical and emotional problems as they get older. So, one of the main jobs in aging is to care for and improve our ties with others.

Redefining Intimacy

As we start the *Third Act*, our understanding of intimacy might change. When we were younger, intimacy often meant physical closeness or romantic relationships. But as we get older, emotional and spiritual closeness become just as important, maybe even more so. One of the tasks of aging is to avoid loneliness and isolation by rethinking intimacy, to match our current needs and values and then doing what it takes to make this a part of our life.

For instance, touch, looking into someone's eyes, and deep meaningful conversation each create a deeply satisfying form of closeness and intimacy. It's about creating moments where we connect with others and go beyond surface-level interactions. This can happen with a partner we've had for years, new friends we've made, or even groups that share our personal values and spiritual beliefs.

Dealing with Loss and Feeling Alone

One of the hurdles many of us encounter in our *Third Act* is loss. As we grow older, friends and loved ones move away, change jobs, or pass on. Physical constraints may stop us from joining activities that used to bring us closer to others. Without knowing that it has occurred these losses sneak up on us and result in feelings of loneliness, isolation and depression which rapidly erode our happiness and quality of life.

Yet *Conscious Aging* pushes us to face these losses with poise, allows us to mourn and then recognize the necessity of reaching out and forming new bonds and relationships. Even in tough situations, volunteering, joining new groups, and consistently reaching out to family and friends will help us maintain a sense of connection and belonging.

Reflective Question:

How have your relationships shifted as you've aged? Which ones require more focus and care?

How do you see intimacy now, compared to your younger days? Where can you find it?

What can you do to strengthen and build your connections with others?

How have you responded to losing relationships (through moving, changing activities or death) in your *Third Act*? What new ways to connect and get support are you prepared to practice?

Action Step

Connection Map:

- Draw a map of your current relationships.
- Group them into different types, such as family, friends, community, acquaintances, intimates, and those with new share interests etc.
- For each group, write down one way you can deepen your bond with those people: spend more time together, talk about important things, or just tell them you care.

Progress Tracking

Weekly Connection Check-In:

- Work on improving at least one relationship, from your connection map, each week.
- Write down what you can do to strengthen that relationship and how it will benefit you and them.
- After a month, look back at what you've done it and notice any changes in; how connected you feel, how close you are to others, and your overall feeling of being a "part of life."

CHAPTER 8

GIVING LIFE MEANING AND PURPOSE

FINDING MEANING IN THE THIRD ACT

The *Third Act* presents a major challenge: finding meaning and purpose. As people step away from many outside roles and responsibilities—through retirement, kids leaving home, or physical limits—they often feel lost or unsure about their purpose. Yet, this search for meaning also allows each of us to rethink what matters. During this life stage, the focus often moves from achieving to contributing—from what we can get to what we can give back.

Friedrich Nietzsche once said, "He who has a Why to live for can bear almost any How." Finding this "Why" is a primary goal, of the *Third Act*, which gives direction, satisfaction and a renewed sense of motivation. At this point, a life full of meaning brings joy, newfound enthusiasm, and hope regardless of the obstacles we will face.

PURPOSE-DRIVEN LIVING

Living purposefully doesn't always mean doing big things or starting life changing projects. You can find it in everyday tasks, like phoning someone you care about, helping in your neighborhood, or enjoying a hobby. Each action shows that life has value even in its simplest moments. The aim of the *Third Act* shouldn't be too much to handle. Instead, it should elevate what you value and increase your access to what you want in life.

Many cultures have an idea that reflects this thought. Take the Japanese word ikigai, for example. It means "something to get up for in the morning" or "the joy of always having things to do." At its core, it shows how having a purpose, big or small, gives us drive and makes us feel alive.

Giving Back

As we embrace our *Third Act*, we find it increasing our desire to give back. Moving beyond the self-focused goals of earlier life stages, we turn toward kindness—using our life experiences, skills, and resources to add to something bigger than ourselves. This might show up as participating in charity work, guiding younger people, or seeking to make positive changes in our community. Whatever shape it takes, the wish to give back often becomes a key part of living purposefully in the later years of life.

Reflective Questions:

Where do you experience the strongest feeling of purpose in your life now?

How has your sense of meaning, and what's really important, changed in your Third Act?

How can you contribute to your neighborhood, loved ones or the broader world?

How can you bring greater meaning and value into your everyday life — even in little ways?

Action Step

Purpose Discovery Exercise:

- Write on the experiences, passions, and skills that have shaped your life.
- Create a list of potential ways to give back or pursue meaningful projects.
- Consider starting small, like volunteering for a local cause, helping a loved one by sharing a skill you've developed, mentoring someone younger, or engaging in creative work that brings joy.

PROGRESS TRACKING

Weekly Purpose Reflection:

- Choose a purpose-driven project to work on each week for the next month.
- Write down how working on this purpose made you feel—did it give you a feeling of satisfaction, happiness, or a deeper understanding of who you are and what you want to do more of?
- Track your progress. Write about changes in your sense of meaning and direction.

CHAPTER 9
THE GIFT OF REBIRTH

Embracing Rebirth in the Third Act

As we move through the *Third Act*, rebirth takes center stage. Instead of seeing aging as a time when we just get worse, The Art of *Conscious Aging* paints it as a time to start anew, reinvent ourselves, and find some new dimensions to living. The *Third Act* allows us to let go of old ways of seeing ourselves that might not work for us anymore. It lets us begin a new part of our lives with new energy, clear intention, and a feeling of nearly infinite possibilities.

This rebirth process requires a desire and willingness to give up old ideas, roles, and attachments. It has a transforming effect on a person, like when Jesus said, "Rise, pick up your bed and walk." It is committing to our own spiritual quest — Joseph Campbells Heroes Journey— and like it we must leave the known world (our old ways), face our biggest fears and pass through a period of deep self-reflection that we might "Return with the Elixir" —our unique gift to life.

Renewal Through Creativity and Passion

We can begin to discover this new life, in our *Third Act*, by pursuing creative activities and things we love. This time in our lives allows us to explore interests we forgot long ago, try new hobbies, or jump into creative projects that seemed impossible before because of family, work or lack of time. Getting back in touch with our creative side energizes and renews us and gives us a growing feeling of — happy, joyous and free.

Besides creativity, doing what we love is key in bringing new energy to life. Our passions push us forward, giving our days meaning and excitement. Whether through art, writing, helping in the community, or guiding others, embracing what we love can lead to big personal changes.

Spiritual Rebirth and Transformation

Rebirth in the *Third Act* isn't just about external goals and inner growth. Many say their later years bring them a deeper spiritual connection to the God of their understanding and a stronger link to something bigger than themselves. This spiritual rebirth often leads to peace, calm, and a tangible connection with life on earth and the universe beyond. During this time, it is useful to increase our practice of prayer, meditation, reverence for nature and communion with others to support this truly miraculous process of rebirth that we find ourselves under-going.

Reflective Questions:

What old roles or identities must you relinquish to experience a re-invention or re-birth?

What can you do, on a daily basis, to welcome new beginnings and fresh starts into your life?

What creative hobbies, projects or interests will enhance your sense of purpose and renewal?

How can you deepen your spiritual connection during this stage of life?

Action Step

- Set aside time to think about the parts of your life where you want a fresh start.
- Create a "Rebirth Plan" that lists steps to let go of old roles, try new creative interests, and boost your spiritual habits.
- This plan will guide you as you embrace starting anew throughout your *Third Act.*

Progress Tracking

- For the coming month, keep tabs on your experiences as you implement your Rebirth Plan.
- Each week, think about any changes in your outlook, energy, or feeling of purpose.
- Jot down areas where you feel a fresh sense of happiness or excitement and any hurdles you face.
- Look over your progress at the month's end and tweak your plan if needed to keep encouraging growth and change.

CONCLUSION

As you read through the main book, *The Art of Conscious Aging* you've examined different aspects of aging with awareness. You've learned to let go of who you used to be, to live in the now, and to keep your body and mind healthy through good food and mindful habits. Each part of the book gives you new ideas and real steps to take to enjoy an extraordinary quality of life and sense of well-being during this key time in your life.

The heart of *conscious aging* beats in the present—our only real moment of life. When we focus on knowing ourselves, keeping things in balance, building relationships, and caring for ourselves, we live with purpose and enjoy true happiness. As we get older, we get to think about our past and shape what we'll leave behind for those who come after us.

Keep in mind *Conscious Aging* doesn't stop. It needs you to think, adjust, and be ready to accept the changes that time brings. This *workbook* is just the start of your trip. As you go on, I hope you find spark in quiet times, power in tough spots, and happiness in the simple things you do daily.

By taking this thoughtful view of getting older, we build a life full of purpose and substance—one where our age doesn't define us, but instead makes us known for the wisdom, kindness, and love we share with others.

The Art of *Conscious Aging* asks us to change our thoughts about getting older. It suggests we see our later years as a time to grow, find new meaning, and tap into our potential rather than a period of decline. By embracing this approach, we radically and positively influence how we live our *Third Act*. We discover that life is not over but actually beginning again, anew, if we are; willing to let go of the past, accept the changes that accompany aging, consider that (almost) anything can happen and take a flying leap into the great unknown of our later years with courage, willingness and curiosity. When we do this, it is not a slogan to say, "*the rest of your life can be the best of our life.*"

Please reach out and let us know how you have grown, changed, and benefitted from your explorations in The Art of *Conscious Aging*. Visit our website, join our community, or invite us to witness, support or join you in your Encore Career or newfound life's purpose.

I wish you all the love, happiness and joy that is your birthright, and the true gift of a well-lived Third Act.

Visit us at: www.waynelehrer.com

NOTES

NOTES

NOTES

NOTES

Thank You So Much For Reading & Using

The Art of Conscious Aging Workbook!

I greatly appreciate the time you took to give my book a read. As a small Independent Author/Publisher, it means a lot and I hope that ***The Art of Conscious Aging Workbook*** has made a difference in your personal aging journey.

If you have 60 seconds, hearing your honest feedback on Amazon would mean the world to me. It does wonder for the book, and I love hearing about your experience with it!

To leave your honest review on Amazon:

1. **Go to AMAZON** and search for ***The Art of Conscious Aging***
2. Click on Book, scroll down, near bottom, **Customer Reviews**
3. **Review This Product - Write a Customer Review** (Click)
4. Enter your honest **Review** – stars, headlines & review.

To Learn More About *Conscious Aging*:

If you would just like to discover what we offer at ***The Art of Conscious Aging***, explore Life Coaching or Conscious Aging Coaching, receive information on Workshops, Retreats and our other events and offerings, or reach out with questions, visit at:

www.waynelehrer.com

Made in United States
Cleveland, OH
15 February 2025

14392770R00044